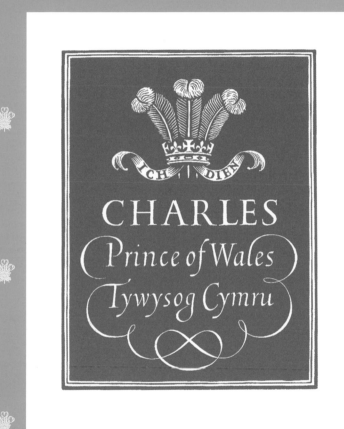

CHARLES

Prince of Wales

Tywysog Cymru

CHARLES
PRINCE OF WALES

A BIRTHDAY SOUVENIR ALBUM

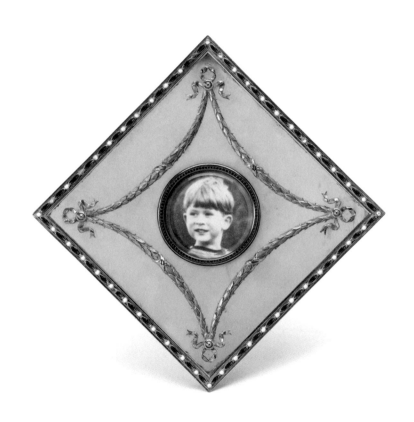

CHARLES
PRINCE OF WALES
A BIRTHDAY SOUVENIR ALBUM

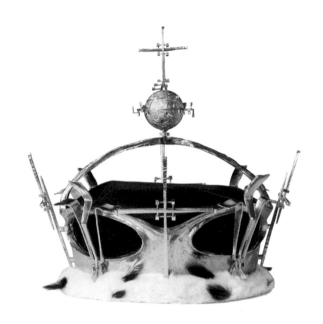

ROYAL COLLECTION PUBLICATIONS

Published by Royal Collection Enterprises Ltd
St James's Palace, London SW1A 1JR

For a complete catalogue of current publications, please write to the address above,
or visit our website on www.royalcollection.org.uk

ISBN 978-1-905686-04-9

British Library Cataloguing in Publication Data:
A catalogue record for this book is available from the British Library.

Compiled by Jane Roberts and Rhian Wong
Designed by Peter Drew of Phrogg Design
Typeset in Garamond
Printed and bound by Studio Fasoli, Verona
Printed on Symbol Tatami White, Fedrigoni, Verona
FSC Mixed Sources Certified Paper CoC-FSC 000010 CQ
Production by Debbie Wayment

Endpapers:
The Prince of Wales's bookplate, designed by Reynolds Stone, 1970

Half title page:
Fabergé frame containing a photograph of Prince Charles,
frame before 1896, photograph *c.*1955 (RCIN 100310)

Title page:
The Prince of Wales's Investiture Coronet,
designed by Louis Osman, 1969 (RCIN 69058)

 The Prince's own words accompanying favourite works in the Royal Collection
are shown in italic, with The Prince of Wales's feathers motif in red.

For further information about The Prince of Wales visit
www.princeofwales.gov.uk

For The Prince's Trust visit
www.princes-trust.org.uk

EARLY YEARS

Prince Charles was born at Buckingham Palace at 9.14 p.m. on the evening of 14 November 1948. He was the first child of Princess Elizabeth and Prince Philip, Duke of Edinburgh. His official title was therefore Prince Charles of Edinburgh. The Prince was also the first grandchild of King George VI and Queen Elizabeth.

The first formal photograph of the Prince was taken by Cecil Beaton in mid-December. In his diary Beaton noted that the Prince 'interrupted a long, contented sleep to do my bidding and open his blue eyes to stare long and wonderingly into the camera lens, the beginning of a lifetime in the glare of public duty'. The brooch worn by Princess Elizabeth in the photograph was a gift from King George VI and Queen Elizabeth, on the Prince's birth.

This hand-written notice announcing the Prince's birth, signed by the royal doctors in attendance, was attached to the railings outside Buckingham Palace. On reading the news, the waiting crowd erupted in joyful celebration. A number of them were wearing the uniform of one or other of the armed services. The British people had suffered much hardship during the six years of the Second World War, and difficult times continued for several years thereafter.

November 14th 1948

The Princess Elizabeth, Duchess of Edinburgh was safely delivered of a Prince at nine fourteen pm today.

Her Royal Highness and her son are both doing well.

The Prince was baptised with the names Charles Philip Arthur George during a private ceremony in the Music Room at Buckingham Palace on 15 December 1948. The christening was conducted by Dr Geoffrey Fisher, the Archbishop of Canterbury. The 'Lily font', made for the baptism of Queen Victoria's first child in 1841, was used for the ceremony.

In the photograph he lies on his mother's lap, between his maternal grandparents (the King and Queen), while his father stands behind. The names of Prince Charles's sponsors (or godparents) are listed on the left page of this specially produced book of the baptism service.

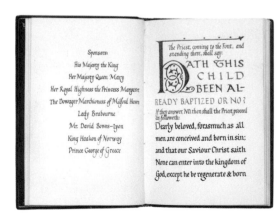

Franz Xaver Winterhalter
The First of May 1851
Oil on canvas

*"There is something deeply touching about the way the aged Duke of Wellington is
shown offering a gift to his little godson and namesake Prince Arthur. This child,
who was Queen Victoria's third son, became Duke of Connaught and was my
mother's godfather, which for me is an extraordinary link back to the middle
of the nineteenth century. I love the way Prince Albert gazes slightly mystically
out of the picture, and that there is a glimpse in the background of his great
achievement, the Crystal Palace which was built to house the Great Exhibition
in that same year – 1851."*

In addition to the principal cake, from which Queen Mary retrieved this floral decoration, several other christening cakes were sent to the Palace. In the photograph Miss Podd – 'icing specialist at McVitie & Price' – is shown putting the finishing touches to one of the cakes.

This silver carousel cake ornament was designed and made by wounded ex-servicemen.

This magnificent late eighteenth-century silver-gilt cup was a christening present from King George III to a godson in 1780. It was acquired by Queen Mary as a christening present for her godson and great-grandson, Prince Charles.

Among the many other gifts to the infant Prince was this set of miniature cutlery in a leather case. The silver pieces have decorated bone-china handles.

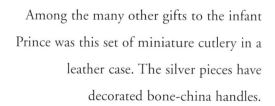

During the Prince's earliest years the family lived at Clarence House, where the Canadian photographer Karsh recorded him with his parents in the summer of 1951.

This copy of *The Tales of Beatrix Potter*, given in 1904 to the four-year-old Elizabeth Bowes Lyon (later Queen Elizabeth The Queen Mother), was a favourite for story-telling in the royal nursery.

Among the first independent formal shots of Prince Charles is this one taken by the photographer Marcus Adams in the same year.

There was a close bond between the Prince and both his maternal grandparents. In 1951 he was photographed with King George VI at Buckingham Palace, a few months before the King's death.

Favoured toys in the royal nursery included this trolley of wooden bricks – the 'Prince Charles Express'.

Much of Prince Charles's early childhood was spent in the company of his sister, Princess Anne, who was born at Clarence House in August 1950. The Duke of Edinburgh was a serving officer in the Royal Navy at the time: note the appropriate decoration on the Prince's pram cover.

On the death of King George VI in February 1952, the Prince's mother succeeded as Queen Elizabeth II and Prince Charles became heir apparent. He also became Duke of Cornwall and succeeded to his titles in the peerage of Scotland (including Duke of Rothesay and Lord of the Isles).

The Royal Family habitually spend the late summer at Balmoral Castle in Aberdeenshire. In 1952 The Queen and her young family were photographed at a window, and in 1953 they were shown in the garden.

Hans Holbein the Younger
Sir John Godsalve, c.1532–4
Black and coloured chalks, watercolour and
bodycolour, on paper

*"When I was young I often used to wander around Windsor Castle after the public
had gone. I had a marvellous time exploring the State Apartments, looking at
things that particularly appealed to me. I suppose it was when I was about thirteen
that individual paintings and works of art began to register strongly.*

*"I remember from my earliest visits to the Print Room in the Royal Library being
completely captivated by the Holbein drawings of Henry VIII's courtiers. Like Van
Dyck, you feel that Holbein saw right into the character of his sitters. Godsalve's
wariness is so well and so economically captured."*

19

In July 1958 it was announced that
The Queen had created her son Prince of
Wales and Earl of Chester, and that his formal
investiture would take place at Caernarfon in
a few years' time. This photograph, taken the
day after the announcement, shows the Prince
returning to school from church. He was a
pupil at his father's old school – Cheam,
near Newbury – from September 1957.

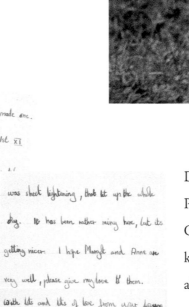

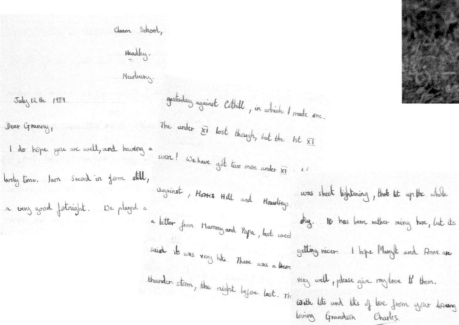

Cheam School,
Headley.
Newbury.

July 12th 1959.

Dear Granny,

I do hope you are well, and having a lovely time. I am second in form still, a very good fortnight. We played a

yesterday against Cothill, in which I made one. The under XI lost though, but the 1st XI won! We have got two more under XI, against, Horris Hill and Hawtreys. a letter from Mummy and Papa, last week said it was very hot. There was a big thunder-storm, the night before last. Th

was sheet lightening, that lit up the whole sky. It has been rather rainy here, but its getting nicer. I hope Margrit and Anne are very well, please give my love to them. With lots and lots of love from your loving Grandson Charles.

During The Queen and
Prince Philip's prolonged visit to
Canada in 1959, Prince Charles
kept his grandmother informed
about news from school.

Among the Prince's school exercise books from his time at Cheam is this history notebook dated July 1960. It is open at an account (with plan) of the Battle of Hastings in 1066.

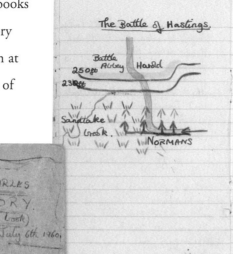

The Prince's geometry set accompanied him throughout his school years. He inscribed his name '*P. CHARLES*' on the wooden ruler.

In addition to his academic work, the Prince took part in outdoor activities in the school holidays. He rode with his mother, and was taught to shoot, fish, ski, play polo and sail by his father.

In August 1957 Prince Charles took part in his first yacht race, in the sailing boat *Bluebottle* at Cowes. Prince Philip is shown here at the tiller, accompanied by Uffa Fox and the sailing master (Lieutenant Commander Easton), with the 8-year-old Prince Charles.

Prince Charles also learnt to skate, at the Richmond Ice Rink, where in March 1962 he received a Certificate of Merit, Preliminary Class Standard.

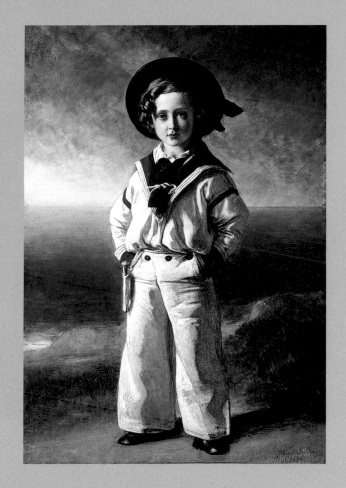

Franz Xaver Winterhalter
Albert Edward, Prince of Wales
(later King Edward VII), 1846
Oil on canvas

"It seems to me that Winterhalter really understood how to paint children: he captures the young Prince effortlessly and most charmingly. He has shown him as a boy of five, standing with hands in the pockets of the new sailor suit that his mother Queen Victoria had had made for him. The Queen kept the picture at Osborne, where I think it was probably painted, reminding her of happy days sailing with Prince Albert on the Royal Yacht."

23

In May 1962 Prince Charles began his first term at his senior school, Gordonstoun, near Elgin in Morayshire. His father had been one of the first pupils there, under the founding Headmaster Kurt Hahn in the 1930s.

During his five years at Gordonstoun, Prince Charles participated in The Duke of Edinburgh Award scheme, founded by his father in 1956 to challenge young people to personal achievement and fulfilment. After undertaking a number of expeditions (including one to Glen Muick in July 1963), the Prince was awarded his first certificate. He received his Silver Award in December 1965.

After the performance, Eric Anderson, Assistant Master of Gordonstoun from 1964 to 1966 (and later Headmaster, then Provost, of Eton), presented Prince Charles with this copy of Palgrave's poetry anthology, *The Golden Treasury*.

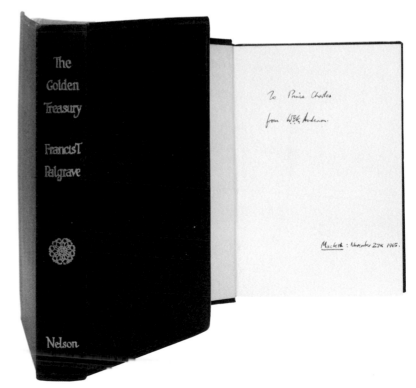

At Gordonstoun Prince Charles took part in a number of school plays and in November 1965 he played the lead in a production of Shakespeare's *Macbeth*. The photograph records Macbeth's soliloquy in Act II, Scene 1 'Is this a dagger which I see before me...'

While there, the Prince joined in a school trip to Papua New Guinea. He was to revisit the island nine years later, as The Queen's representative during its independence celebrations.

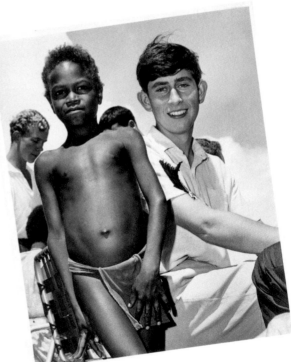

Between February and July 1966 Prince Charles was an exchange student at Timbertop, the remote outback annexe of Geelong Church of England Grammar School in the foothills of the Great Dividing Range in Victoria, Australia. The emphasis there is on practical projects and outdoor activities, in addition to academic work.

Two years later the veteran photographer Cecil Beaton photographed the Prince at the entrance to the White Drawing Room, Buckingham Palace – to mark the Prince's twentieth birthday. This was Beaton's last royal sitting.

After his time in Australia Prince Charles returned to Gordonstoun for his final year, from September 1966 to July 1967. In his last term he was elected Guardian, or Head Boy, and took A-levels in History and French. On the Prince's eighteenth birthday in November 1966 he became eligible to serve as a Counsellor of State – one of those appointed to stand in for the Sovereign during her absence abroad, or through illness. A number of photographs of His Royal Highness were released to the press on this occasion. Some – like the one above – show him in the relaxed setting of Balmoral.

In October 1967 Prince Charles went up to Trinity College, Cambridge, following in the footsteps of his great-great-grandfather, King Edward VII. In addition to his academic studies, The Prince took part in the musical and theatrical life of the university, played polo and began flying lessons with the RAF – and also undertook some public duties.

Trinity College Great Court.

CAMBRIDGE University ALMANACK, 1846.

University holidays were divided between the different royal residences – including Windsor, where The Prince was photographed by Lord Snowdon, studying in the Royal Library.

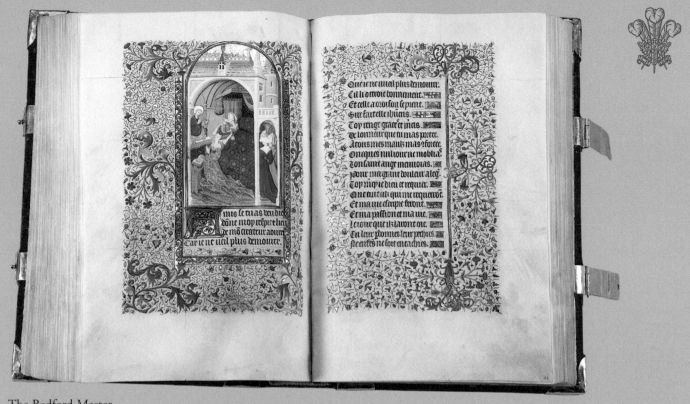

The Bedford Master

Margaret of Burgundy, praying to St Margaret, in the Sobieski Book of Hours, c.1420–25

Manuscript on vellum; bound in red velvet with gold mounts

bearing the initials of John Sobieski, King of Poland

"I used to spend hours in the Library when I was younger and would lose myself looking at the tiny, colourful and exquisitely painted scenes in this wonderful Book of Hours. I find the provenance of the book very intriguing too: it came from the court of Burgundy to the King of Poland and descended to the last of the Stuarts, Cardinal York, who bequeathed it to George IV."

Prince Charles spent his first year at Cambridge reading Archaeology and Anthropology, and his second and third years reading History. Public interest in The Prince's living accommodation at Cambridge led to the release of a number of photographs of his college rooms, including the kitchen.

After three years of study, in June 1970 the Prince was awarded the degree of Bachelor of Arts. In August 1975 he received the degree of Master of Arts, which was conferred on His Royal Highness in person at the Senate House in Cambridge.

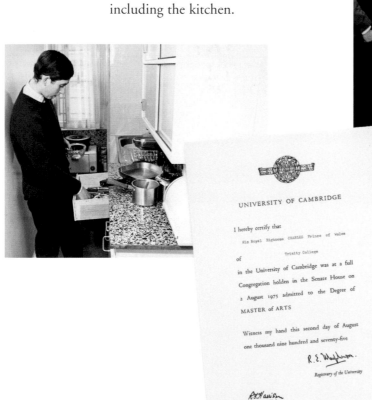

By the late 1960s Prince Charles was playing polo regularly and in 1968 won a Half Blue playing for Cambridge University.

Prince Charles was encouraged to take up polo by both his father and his great-uncle Earl Mountbatten of Burma, who gave The Prince a copy of his *Introduction to Polo* – inscribed with his pseudonym 'Marco'.

This silver-mounted polo ball was used by The Prince to score a goal in the Prince Louis Cup in Malta. In the 1970s Prince Charles played for the Royal Navy and received the Rundle Cup (upper left) from Lord Mountbatten shortly before the latter's death. The Prince had captained the victorious Navy team in the annual match against the Army.

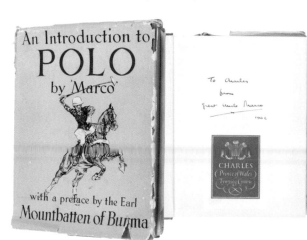

Prince Charles's second summer term at university was spent away from Cambridge, at the University College of Wales Aberystwyth, where he studied Welsh language and history.

In May 1969 he made his first public speech in Welsh, on the final day of the Urdd Gobaith Cymru (Welsh League of Youth) Eisteddfod at Aberystwyth.

PRINCE OF WALES

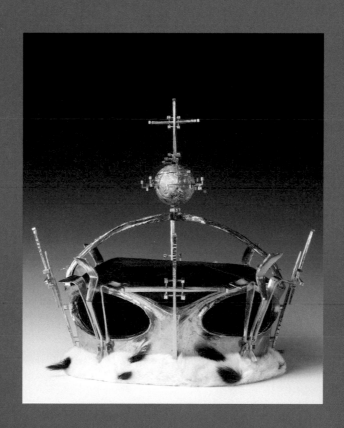

The Prince's role within the United Kingdom was established when he was formally invested as Prince of Wales. This took place in a ceremony at Caernarfon Castle on 1 July 1969. The Prince is the twenty-first English Prince of Wales and can trace his descent to the Welsh Princes through the Tudor dynasty.

INVESTITURE
OF HIS ROYAL HIGHNESS
THE PRINCE OF WALES
ARWISGIAD
EI UCHELDER BRENHINOL
TYWYSOG CYMRU

Caernarvon 1969 Caernarfon

The ceremony was directed by the Constable of Caernarfon Castle, Lord Snowdon. A number of innovatory features – including the blue (rather than red) wax seal of The Prince's Letters Patent – were introduced into the investiture ceremony. The Prince of Wales's motto is 'Ich Dien', meaning 'I serve'.

A new diamond- and emerald-set gold
investiture coronet was created for the
occasion, to the design of Louis Osman. After
The Queen had placed the coronet on the
head of the new Prince of Wales, and the
investiture cloak had been placed on his
shoulders, The Prince pledged his allegiance
with these words: 'I, Charles, Prince of Wales,
do become your liege man of life and limb.'

After a short religious service, The Queen and
Duke of Edinburgh led The Prince to Queen
Eleanor's Gate, overlooking Caernarfon's
Castle Square, and presented him to the
crowds below.

This formal portrait of The Prince of Wales in his investiture robes was taken by Norman Parkinson. The investiture coronet and cloak were specially made for the 1969 investiture. The clasps of the cloak, and the sword, rod and ring, were created for the investiture of the future King Edward VIII as Prince of Wales in 1911.

An important part of the investiture ceremony was the reading of the Loyal Address from the people of Wales by Sir Ben Bowen Thomas, President of the University College of Wales. This copy of the Welsh and English text of the Address was designed and bound at Newport College of Art and Design, for presentation to His Royal Highness.

The Prince's response was delivered in Welsh using this typescript text. In translation, the opening passage reads: 'The words of your address have certainly touched me deeply and I can assure you I have taken note of the hopes expressed in them. It is, indeed, my firm intention to associate myself in word and deed with as much of the life of the Principality as possible – and what a Principality!'

A LOYAL ADDRESS
PRESENTED ON BEHALF OF
THE PEOPLE OF WALES
TO THE PRINCE OF WALES
IN CAERNARVON CASTLE
ON THE FIRST DAY OF JULY 1969
BY SIR BEN BOWEN THOMAS
PRESIDENT OF
THE UNIVERSITY COLLEGE OF WALES
ABERYSTWYTH

INVESTITURE REPLY.

Mae eich anerchiad wedi fy nghyffwrdd yn ddwys / a gallaf eich sicrhau fy mod wedi cymryd sylw o'r gobeithion amlygwyd ynddyn nhw. Yn wir. / rwy'n bwriadu cysylltu fy hun o ddifrif mewn gair a gweithred â chymaint o fywyd y Dywysogaeth a'r fath Dywysogaeth ydy ni! – ag a fydd yn bosibl.

'Roeddwn i'n teimlo cryn dipyn o falchder / ac emosiwn wrth dderbyn y symbolau hyn o'm swydd yn y gaer odidog hon. Lle ni allai neb beidio a theimlo rhyw gyffrô yn awyrgylch ei gwychder hynafol.

According to the Statutes of the Order of the Garter, Prince Charles automatically became a Knight of the Garter on his appointment as Prince of Wales in July 1958. However, he was not invested and installed as a Garter Knight until 17 June 1968.

The Order of the Garter, founded by King Edward III in 1348, is Britain's senior Order of chivalry. The original members were the Sovereign, the Prince of Wales (Edward, the Black Prince) and 24 Companions. The seat of the Order is St George's Chapel, Windsor Castle. The Garter insignia (at left) worn by The Prince of Wales includes the diamond star given by Queen Victoria to her eldest son, Albert Edward, Prince of Wales (later King Edward VII) and the diamond sash badge given to King George V by the 'Georges of the Empire'. The band – or garter – worn around the Prince's leg is shown below.

The Prince's Bath collar (left) was originally made for George IV, who greatly enlarged the membership of the Order at the time of the Napoleonic wars. The Prince's diamond breast star formerly belonged to George, Duke of Cambridge, a grandson of George III.

The Order of the Bath, re-established in 1725, is the premier meritorious Order. It consists of the Sovereign, a Great Master and three classes of members, each class having both a civil and a military division. The seat of the Order is Westminster Abbey. The Prince of Wales is shown here following his installation as Great Master of the Order in 1975, wearing the Great Master's crowned neck badge.

The Prince of Wales performs a number of functions in support of The Queen's role as Commander-in-Chief of the armed forces. His Royal Highness's military career commenced immediately after he left university with a six-month period at the Royal Air Force College at Cranwell, learning to fly jet aircraft. The Prince's Flying Log Book (below) records his flights in July 1971, during the final weeks of his training.

In August 1971, Flight Lieutenant The Prince of Wales obtained his RAF wings. Shortly before, an RAF photographer had captured The Prince on a solo training flight in formation with his instructor, Squadron Leader (later Air Chief Marshal Sir Richard) Johns. Squadron Leader Johns was asked to produce a written account of The Prince's flying instruction. This was published as *Wings for the Prince of Wales* in 1973. The Prince's current rank in the RAF is Air Chief Marshal.

In September 1971 The Prince of Wales enrolled as Sub-Lieutenant at the Britannia Royal Naval College, Dartmouth, where his father had also trained. The Prince's training and service in the Royal Navy – the senior service – was probably decided in his early years.

After completing his course at Dartmouth in November, The Prince joined the guided-missile destroyer HMS *Norfolk*, on which he served until July 1972. The Queen paid a visit to HMS *Norfolk* during his service.

In 1973 His Royal Highness was promoted to acting Lieutenant, while serving on the frigate HMS *Minerva*. In January 1974 he was appointed to another frigate, HMS *Jupiter*. In this photograph he is shown launching a helicopter, as Flight Deck Officer on *Jupiter*.

Between August and October 1974 The Prince qualified as a helicopter pilot at the Royal Naval Air Station, Yeovilton, Somerset.

After serving on the commando carrier HMS *Hermes*, part of 845 Naval Air Squadron, in September 1975 The Prince of Wales undertook the Lieutenant's course at Greenwich and in the following February took command of the coastal mine-hunter HMS *Bronington*.

During this command he received visits from The Queen, The Duke of Edinburgh (Admiral of the Fleet), and also from Prince Andrew, a future naval officer.

The Prince of Wales was in command of *Bronington* throughout the remainder of 1976 – sporting a naval 'full set' for part of the time.

His Royal Highness left the navy in December 1976. Since 2006 he has held the rank of Admiral in the Royal Navy. The uniform details shown here are from his Royal Navy ceremonial tailcoat No. 1.

Sir Thomas Lawrence
Arthur Wellesley,
1st Duke of Wellington,
1814–15
Oil on canvas

"I find it almost impossible to choose one Lawrence out of that great ensemble in the Waterloo Chamber at Windsor. What an amazing commission it was – to travel round the courts of Europe, painting all the allied sovereigns and politicians after the final overthrow of Napoleon at Waterloo. But in the end, I think the greatest image is that of the Duke of Wellington himself, standing with the Sword of State against a backdrop of St Paul's Cathedral."

Since 1975 The Prince has been Colonel of the Welsh Guards, one of the five British regiments of Foot Guards. At the Trooping the Colour ceremony each June, The Queen's Colour of a different Foot Guards battalion is 'trooped' to celebrate the Sovereign's official birthday. In 1981 it was the turn of the 1st Battalion, Welsh Guards. Riding alongside The Queen and The Duke of Edinburgh, The Prince of Wales wore his Welsh Guards tunic and bearskin for the ceremony. The white-green-white plume (also worn by The Queen) is clearly identifiable.

In 1977 The Prince of Wales was appointed Colonel-in-Chief of the Parachute Regiment, after undertaking a parachute course to justify his wearing their famous beret and wings badge.

Both Prince Harry and Prince William are now serving officers in the Army. Their proud father is seen with them at Prince Harry's passing out parade at Sandhurst in April 2006.

In 2007 His Royal Highness was promoted to the rank of General in the British Army.

The Prince of Wales has no formal constitutional role but devotes much of his active life to supporting The Queen through public duties. He undertook his first official royal duty while still a schoolboy at Gordonstoun: in June 1965 he attended a student garden party at the Palace of Holyroodhouse, The Queen's official residence in Edinburgh.

While an undergraduate at Cambridge, in December 1968 he accompanied other members of the Royal Family to the opening of the new Royal Mint at Llantrisant, Glamorgan. The Prince of Wales personally struck these 2p pieces. Although struck in 1968, the coins bear the date 1971, when they became legal tender as part of Britain's decimal currency.

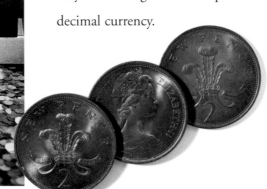

Increasingly during recent years, The Prince of Wales has shared the duties of conducting investitures with Her Majesty The Queen, at Buckingham Palace and Holyroodhouse. On these occasions the achievements of individuals throughout the United Kingdom are recognised. In 2003 he invested the actress Helen Mirren with the insignia of Dame of the British Empire. Three years later Dame Helen won international renown with her award-winning performance in the film *The Queen*.

The Prince of Wales's public duties have continued to concentrate primarily on the United Kingdom and Commonwealth countries. In The Queen's Golden Jubilee year – 2002 – The Prince was appointed to the Order of Merit, in recognition of his exceptional service. The Order is within the personal gift of the Sovereign.

Over the last sixty years many British dominions and territories have become independent states. At each independence ceremony The Queen is represented by a senior member of the Royal Family. Prince Charles performed this duty for the first time in October 1970, when Fiji became an independent realm within the Commonwealth.

This watercolour shows the Royal Yacht *Britannia* in Hong Kong harbour in July 1997, where it served as the base for the royal party following the handover of the former British Protectorate. It was painted by Susannah Fiennes, the artist invited to accompany The Prince to Hong Kong. He had reintroduced the practice of taking an artist on overseas tours in 1985, resulting in many memorable – and very personal – records.

The Prince has visited most Commonwealth countries at least once, and has revisited a number on several occasions. In February 2000 he visited Trinidad, Tobago, Guyana and Jamaica. He was accompanied on that visit by the artist Mary Anne Aytoun Ellis, who produced this fine tempera and ink study during the tour.

Following his time at Timbertop in 1966, The Prince of Wales has made thirteen return visits to Australia. In November 1977 he attended the Tweed River Agricultural Society's Silver Jubilee at Murwillumbah, south of Brisbane.

Four years earlier, His Royal Highness had been created Knight of the Order of Australia (AK). The Order was instituted by The Queen in 1975, but the rank of Knight or Dame was discontinued in 1986. The Prince of Wales is one of only three living AKs.

His Royal Highness also has long-standing links with Africa. The ebony box containing gold cufflinks and tie-pin were given to him during The Queen's visit to Ghana in 1961. The Prince of Wales paid his own first visit to Ghana in 1977.

In England in the mid-1970s The Prince of Wales met the writer and conservationist Laurens van der Post, and in 1977 joined him on safari in Africa. In 1986 Van der Post (who had been knighted in 1981) sent The Prince a proof copy of his book *A Walk with a White Bushman* and in the following year The Prince commissioned a portrait of him from the artist Derek Hill. Sir Laurens, who died in 1996, was godfather to Prince William of Wales.

In October and November 1997 The Prince
of Wales paid an official visit to Swaziland
and South Africa. He attended the coronation
of King Letsie III in Lesotho before
proceeding to Mahlamba Ndlopfu, Pretoria,
for lunch with Nelson Mandela, President of
South Africa from 1994 to 1999. Under
Mandela's Presidency, South Africa regained
its membership of the Commonwealth, which
it had left in 1961.

The Prince was accompanied on this visit by
the artist Robbie Wraith, who made these
studies while the royal party was passing
through Cape Town.

"I have always found the Tribuna especially appealing. Even though I did not actually visit Italy and see the Uffizi until my late thirties, I felt I had at least had a first introduction to Florence, thanks to Zoffany. I love the massing of pictures in that marvellous room, and the way Zoffany so brilliantly celebrates the Grand Tour and the art of collecting. It was painted for Queen Charlotte, and for her and George III it was a substitute for an actual visit – sadly for them, they never went to Italy."

The Prince of Wales first visited Italy in 1985 and has returned on several occasions. Peter Kuhfeld's view of the *Loggia dei Lanzi, Florence,* was a fiftieth birthday present from the artist in 1998.

Johan Zoffany, *The Tribuna of the Uffizi,* 1772–8. Oil on canvas

His Royal Highness has also travelled several times to Russia and to countries in the former Soviet Union. In 1991 he paid an official visit to Czechoslovakia. The tour artist for that visit was John Sergeant, who painted this view of the skyline of Hradçany in the historic centre of Prague.

Leena, a university student in Turkmenistan, was drawn by Emma Sergeant during The Prince's tour of the Ukraine and the Central Asian Republics in November 1996. On the same visit His Royal Highness received the insignia of the Breast Plate of the President of the Republic of Kazakhstan, shown above.

The Prince of Wales has paid several visits to
North America. He participated in the
celebrations of the Blackfoot Confederacy in
July 1977, a hundred years after the signing
of their original treaty with the Canadian
Government during the reign of Queen
Victoria. At Gleichen, Alberta, he was made
an honorary chief and was dubbed Mekaisto
– Red Crow.

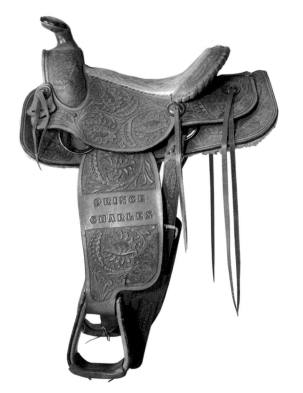

In the course of his visit he was
given this magnificent saddle by
the Blood Tribe – members of
the Blackfoot Confederacy.

The Prince first visited the United States in 1970, when he stayed at the White House as the guest of President Nixon. In 1981 – shortly before his wedding – he was the guest of President Reagan. The President's wedding present to The Prince and Princess of Wales was an engraved crystal bowl on a malachite base.

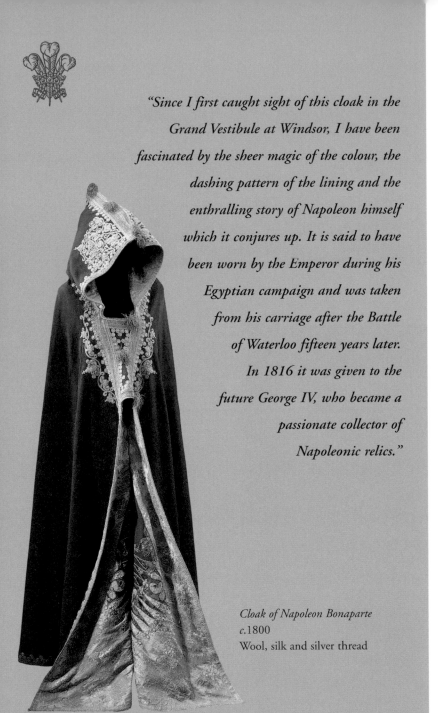

"Since I first caught sight of this cloak in the Grand Vestibule at Windsor, I have been fascinated by the sheer magic of the colour, the dashing pattern of the lining and the enthralling story of Napoleon himself which it conjures up. It is said to have been worn by the Emperor during his Egyptian campaign and was taken from his carriage after the Battle of Waterloo fifteen years later. In 1816 it was given to the future George IV, who became a passionate collector of Napoleonic relics."

Cloak of Napoleon Bonaparte
*c.*1800
Wool, silk and silver thread

In the course of The Prince's visit to Egypt in 1995 he received the Order of St Catherine of Mount Sinai from the President. The artist Emma Sergeant was present throughout the tour. In addition to sketching in the Cairo Museum, she made a number of drawings from imagination.

The Prince of Wales has established close links with Saudi Arabia and other Gulf States. In March 2006, in the course of an official visit that commenced in Egypt and proceeded to Saudi Arabia and India, he received this gold and quartz model of a desert scene from King Abdullah of Saudi Arabia.

His Royal Highness received the Kuwaiti Order, Mubarak Al Kabir, in 1995. The insignia had been redesigned in 1991, following the liberation of Kuwait.

"*The links between this country and India are strong and deep and on my visits I have always been very aware of the rich diversity of the artistic heritage of the subcontinent. Queen Victoria, as Empress of India, received many splendid gifts from India, and among the most captivating for me is this diamond-encrusted belt set with Mughal emeralds which had belonged to Maharajah Ranjit Singh, ruler of the Punjab.*"

Indian (Lahore)
*Emerald belt of Maharajah Sher Singh, c.*1840
Emeralds, diamonds, pearls, gold, fabric,
silver-gilt thread

India is a country close to The Prince's heart. He paid a two-week visit in November 1980, in the course of which a local photographer created this image – in the shape of a leaf

FAMILY LIFE

The Prince's parents and grandmother have provided the foundations for his life and work. This portrait of The Queen was a study for the painting by Michael Noakes commissioned by the Corporation of London to celebrate Her Majesty's Silver Wedding anniversary in November 1972. The portrait of The Duke of Edinburgh by Bryan Organ dates from 1983.

The Prince commissioned this set of boxes from the silversmith Gerald Benney as a Silver Wedding present for his parents.

The Prince grew up in a tight-knit family, with two much younger brothers. At Easter 1965 the Royal Family was recorded in the grounds of Frogmore House, Windsor, around Prince Edward's pram.

Four years later, Prince Charles, Princess Anne and Prince Edward were photographed on go-karts in the Royal Mews.

The Old Man of Lochnagar – set in the landscape of the Balmoral estate – began as a story invented by The Prince to entertain Princes Andrew and Edward. It was first published in 1980 and was subsequently made into an animated film, a musical stage play, and a ballet. The Prince's Trust – founded by The Prince of Wales in 1976 – has benefited substantially from the book.

Landseer's painting of Queen Victoria's dogs Hector, Nero and Dash – with the parrot Lory – was painted in 1838. It was chosen by His Royal Highness to hang in the Dining Room at Clarence House, his London residence. The photograph of The Prince at Balmoral with an adoring golden Labrador, Harvey, was released to celebrate The Prince's thirtieth birthday in November 1978.

"Landseer's ability to capture the likeness of favourite animals was one of his accomplishments as a painter that Queen Victoria most admired. This dazzling image of Prince Albert's beloved greyhound, Eos, hangs at Balmoral where it greets us on our way to and from the dining room, and is a cheerful reminder of the fact that our family has always had a tremendous love of dogs."

Tigga, a Jack Russell terrier, was The Prince of Wales's close companion from 1984 until her death in 2002. She was portrayed by the sculptress Angela Conner in 1995.

Sir Edwin Landseer, *Eos*, 1841. Oil on canvas

"I greatly admire the acute and sympathetic way Stubbs observes the coachman and the groom – as well as (of course) the wonderful rendering of the horses. He misses nothing."

George Stubbs, *The Prince of Wales's Phaeton,* 1793. Oil on canvas

The Prince of Wales shares a love of horses with The Queen and other members of the Royal Family. He learnt to ride at an early age and continues to keep a number of horses at Highgrove.

During the 1980s The Prince rode in several competitive races. On his horse Allibar he came second in the Clun Handicap Chase at Ludlow in 1980, as shown (as number 5) in the above photograph, and as recorded on this silver-mounted inkwell.

The close relationship between man and horse, shown so subtly by Landseer in his equestrian portrait of Queen Victoria (now hanging at Clarence House), is also captured in this photograph of The Prince of Wales holding his pony's head during a break in a polo match in the 1970s.

"Queen Victoria loved Landseer's work and there are many wonderful portraits by him in the Collection. His paintings are usually highly finished but for some reason he left this one only partly completed. I particularly love the spontaneity and freshness that you see in an unfinished work and I think this is what also appealed to my grandmother, who bought the painting in the late 1940s."

Sir Edwin Landseer
Queen Victoria on horseback, c.1841
Oil on canvas

The engagement of The Prince of Wales to Lady Diana Spencer was announced in February 1981 and their marriage took place at St Paul's Cathedral on 29 July 1981. Lady Diana, who was thirteen years younger than Prince Charles, had been brought up close to Sandringham House in Norfolk and had known The Prince since her early childhood.

The wedding was a spectacular occasion, witnessed by vast crowds in London and transmitted by television to millions of viewers around the world.

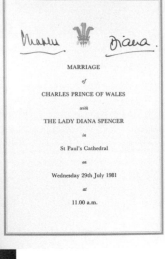

MARRIAGE

of

CHARLES PRINCE OF WALES

with

THE LADY DIANA SPENCER

in

St Paul's Cathedral

on

Wednesday 29th July 1981

at

11.00 a.m.

The silver Welsh dragon was a wedding present from the Welsh Guards to their Colonel.

After The Prince and Princess of Wales had returned by horse-drawn carriage to Buckingham Palace, a number of formal photographs were taken in the Throne Room. When the other participants had dispersed, Lord Lichfield took this photograph of the bride and groom alone. He commented: 'It is rare to picture a bride seated like this but the Princess of Wales's dress made a marvellous frame for such a pose.'

The Prince and Princess of Wales began their honeymoon in Gibraltar where they embarked on a Mediterranean cruise on the Royal Yacht *Britannia*.

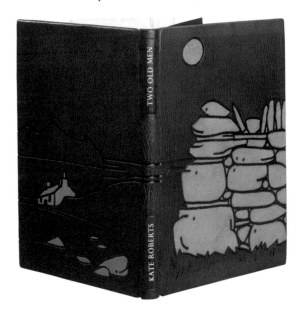

Other gifts included a number of small Lalique crystal dishes and this Fabergé desk seal incorporating the figure of a frog.

Among the quantities of wedding presents sent to the Prince and Princess was this specially bound book, printed by the re-established Gregynog Press. It was a gift from the University of Wales, of which The Prince is Chancellor.

The Prince and Princess's first child, Prince William, was born in June 1982. Like Prince Charles, he was christened at Buckingham Palace. The group photograph shows the infant Prince with his parents and godparents immediately after the ceremony, on 4 August 1982.

The London residence of The Prince and Princess of Wales was an apartment in Kensington Palace, where this photograph was taken in December 1982.

At the time of Prince William's second birthday in June 1984, the press were invited to a photographic session in the garden at Kensington Palace. There The Prince of Wales explained the workings of a cine-camera to his son.

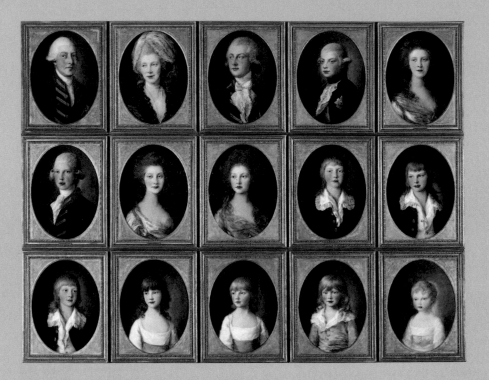

"Gainsborough was insistent about the way his portraits of George III and his family should be hung when they were shown at the Royal Academy – all together in a block and at eye level. He manages to convey the widely differing personalities of the sitters so well – even the recently deceased little Prince Alfred (bottom right). Two of the fifteen children of the King and Queen were not painted: Frederick Duke of York and the yet-to-be-born Princess Amelia. My grandfather re-hung the portraits at Windsor in the late 1940s, using the written instructions Gainsborough gave to the Academy in the 1780s."

Thomas Gainsborough
King George III and his family, 1782–3
Oil on canvas (15 separate canvases)

The Prince and Princess's second child, Harry, was born in September 1984. In the following year he joined his parents and brother on a two-week tour of Italy, based on HMY *Britannia*. Prince William waved from the yacht to the waiting crowds in Venice, while the artist John Ward – who accompanied the royal party throughout this tour – recorded the view of Venice from *Britannia*.

This photograph of the three Princes was taken at Kensington Palace in October 1985.

The house and estate of Highgrove, near
Tetbury in Gloucestershire, was purchased
by the Duchy of Cornwall as the country
residence of The Prince of Wales in 1980.
This watercolour is one of many views of
Highgrove painted by His Royal Highness.

For The Prince and his sons Highgrove has
served as their principal family home. It has
been the scene of a number of family parties
– including His Royal Highness's forty-fifth
birthday party in 1993, for which Toby Ward
painted a special menu card reflecting
The Prince's love of all things Italian.

Many of The Prince of Wales's favourite works of art are kept at Highgrove. These include *The Little Princess* by the Hungarian sculptor László Marton. The Prince first encountered Marton's work during his visit to Hungary in 1990 and received the figurine as a gift in 1993.

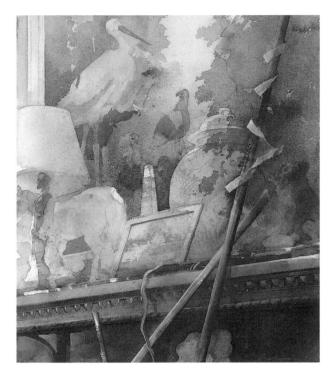

Highgrove is a convenient base for polo-playing at nearby Cirencester. Hugh Buchanan's watercolour records the hall table at Highgrove in 1994. Propped up against the table are two broken polo sticks.

The Prince of Wales is a frequent visitor to
The Queen's private residence in Norfolk,
Sandringham House, with its fine agricultural
and sporting estate. The property – shown
here in The Prince's watercolour of 1991– was
acquired in 1862 for the use of Albert Edward,
Prince of Wales (later King Edward VII).

For much of The Queen's reign, the Royal
Family has celebrated Christmas together at
Sandringham. In early January 1988 Princes
William and Harry were photographed on
one of the old fire engines at Sandringham.

Sandringham is also used by The Prince for
entertaining special-interest groups. These
designs for the menu card for a dinner in
2002 were made by Alec Cobbe.

Among The Prince's favourite pieces of sculpture is this silver St George, commissioned from Alfred Gilbert as a memorial to the Duke of Clarence – the eldest son of Albert Edward, Prince of Wales – who died at Sandringham in 1892. It was later placed in the church at Sandringham.

The principal reception room at Sandringham is the Saloon on the ground floor. This watercolour was painted for The Prince of Wales by Hugh Buchanan in 1986.

The outdoors plays an important part in The Prince's life, whether at Highgrove, Sandringham, Balmoral or Birkhall. The Royal Family's love of picnics dates back to the nineteenth century. In this drawing by the Hungarian artist Mihaly Zichy the future King Edward VII enjoys a break while shooting on Lochnagar in 1877.

The noble bleakness of Lochnagar, with the rapidly changing light and colour, has frequently been painted by The Prince of Wales. This watercolour dates from January 2000.

In the summer of 1971 Lord Lichfield captured Prince Charles greeting his cousin Lady Sarah Armstrong-Jones on the hill above Balmoral. As the photographer explained, it is not a photograph of a Highland Fling but a record of the meeting of two fond relations.

Hugh Buchanan's view of the Library at Balmoral was commissioned by The Prince of Wales in 1986.

Particularly since the death of Queen Elizabeth The Queen Mother in 2002 His Royal Highness has used Birkhall – on the Balmoral estate – as his Scottish residence. The Christmas card (below) shows the Princes in the front porch at Birkhall in 2000.

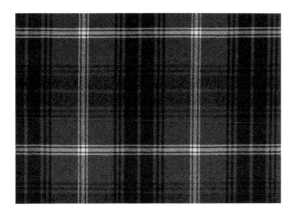

In Scotland The Prince's title is the Duke of Rothesay. His Royal Highness has his own tartan (shown here) – one of a number available for his use.

Carl Haag
The fording of the Poll Tarff on 9 October 1861, 1865
Watercolour on paper

"There are a great many watercolours by Carl Haag in the Royal Collection and I share Queen Victoria's enthusiasm for him as a brilliant draughtsman and colourist. This image, which I find especially evocative, hangs at Balmoral and epitomises to me life in the Highlands as it was in Queen Victoria's time – in some ways not so greatly changed today. It shows an expedition led by the Queen and Prince Albert crossing a ford at Blair Atholl, two months before Prince Albert's death."

The Prince and his sons were at Balmoral in late August 1997 at the time of the tragic death of Diana, Princess of Wales, in a road accident in Paris. Before the Princess's funeral at Westminster Abbey on 6 September, The Prince walked behind her coffin with his father, his two sons, and the Princess's brother Earl Spencer.

Although The Prince and Princess were divorced in August 1996, Diana had continued to live at Kensington Palace as a member of the Royal Family, carrying out public work for a large number of charities.

Following his separation from the Princess of
Wales in late 1992, The Prince occupied an
apartment in St James's Palace. After the death
in 2002 of Queen Elizabeth The Queen
Mother, her London home, Clarence House,
became once again the London base for
The Prince's family life, and also his office.

Edward Halliday's painting (*Maundy
Thursday 1952*) shows the Royal Family at
Clarence House during The Prince's early
childhood, before the move to Buckingham
Palace in 1953.

The Prince moved to the refurbished Clarence House in June 2003, shortly before the fiftieth anniversary of The Queen's Coronation. On that occasion a photograph was taken of three generations of the Royal Family, before a celebratory dinner. Over a thousand guests are entertained at Clarence House each year and during the summer months the ground-floor rooms are open to the public. Among the few obvious changes made since 2002 has been the creation of a new formal garden, designed by The Prince himself.

Clarence House remains largely furnished with Queen Elizabeth's collection. This watercolour by the Russian artist Savely Sorine was painted in 1923, the year of the sitter's marriage to the future King George VI. It hangs in the library, opposite the portrait of Princess Elizabeth.

William Nicholson's *The Gold Jug*, painted in 1937, was purchased from the artist in 1942 and hangs in The Prince's Sitting Room at Clarence House.

The watercolour portrait of The Queen when Princess Elizabeth was painted by Sorine in 1947, to mark the Princess's twenty-first birthday, and the year of her marriage. It is a companion piece to the portrait of Queen Elizabeth (opposite) painted twenty-four years earlier.

Duncan Grant's *Still life with Matisse* was a late work, dating from the artist's ninth decade. It was purchased by Queen Elizabeth in 1973 and, like the Nicholson, hangs in His Royal Highness's Sitting Room at Clarence House.

In April 2005 The Prince of Wales married Mrs Camilla Parker-Bowles in a private ceremony at the Windsor Guildhall. On marriage, the bride was given the title Duchess of Cornwall. The newly-married couple are shown here outside St George's Chapel immediately after the Service of Prayer and Dedication following their civil marriage.

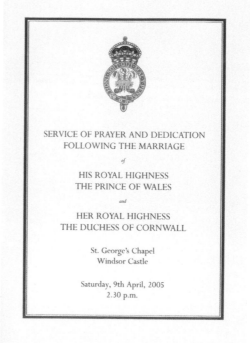

SERVICE OF PRAYER AND DEDICATION
FOLLOWING THE MARRIAGE

of

HIS ROYAL HIGHNESS
THE PRINCE OF WALES

and

HER ROYAL HIGHNESS
THE DUCHESS OF CORNWALL

St. George's Chapel
Windsor Castle

Saturday, 9th April, 2005
2.30 p.m.

This portrait of the Duchess of Cornwall was a wedding present to Their Royal Highnesses from the artist, Mary Anne Aytoun Ellis.

The diamond-set Fabergé cigarette case was a present to King Edward VII from Mrs Keppel in 1908. After the King's death it was returned by Queen Alexandra to Mrs Keppel, who in turn gave it to Queen Mary in 1936. The Duchess of Cornwall is the great-granddaughter of Mrs Keppel.

This portrait of The Prince of Wales by Andrew Ratcliffe
was painted at Kensington Palace in 1985.

INTERESTS
AND CHARITIES

The Duchy of Cornwall –

established by Edward III in 1337 –

lies at the heart of The Prince of Wales's life

and work. The Duchy owns around 55,000

hectares of land in 23 counties, mostly in the

south-west of England. Its principal activity is

the sustainable and commercial management

of that land.

On reaching his twenty-first birthday in

1969, The Prince became entitled to the

full income of the Duchy and took over

its management. He uses a substantial

proportion of that income to fund his public

and charitable work.

In 1992 a new design for the Duchy's crest,

with the motto *Houmout* (an obscure

Flemish word meaning either 'honour' or

'high-spirited'), was commissioned from the

artist John Sergeant.

In 1992 The Prince founded a company called Duchy Originals. In his own words: 'I wanted to demonstrate that it was possible to produce food of the highest quality, working in harmony with the environment and nature, using the best ingredients and adding value through expert production.'

The first product was Oaten Biscuits, launched in 1992. These were made from wheat and oats grown organically on the Home Farm at Highgrove.

There are now over two hundred different products, and Duchy Originals generates more than £1 million profit each year. All the profits are passed to The Prince's Charities Foundation.

The Prince has been keenly interested in farming and the environment for many decades. He delivered his first speech on the environment in 1970 and twenty years later his BBC documentary – *Earth in Balance* – was transmitted, urging a reassessment of our relationship with the natural world.

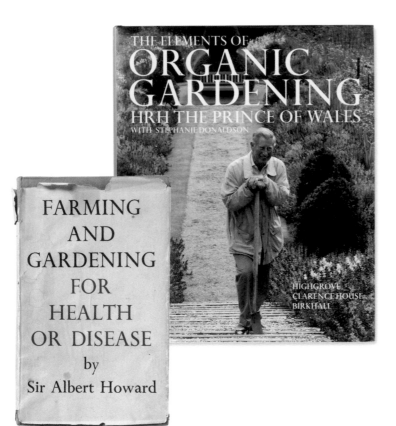

In his cultivation of the land at Highgrove he has espoused organic principles. For these he is indebted to the work of the agricultural botanist Sir Albert Howard, who worked in India from the 1920s and was an early critic of chemical sprays and fertilisers.

The Prince of Wales is a 'hands-on' gardener, with his own favourite gardening gloves, secateurs and hedging tools.

Many works of art in The Prince's different residences reflect his love of the natural world. These pieces from an early Chelsea botanical service were part of Queen Elizabeth's collection, while Lucian Freud's *Small fern* was a fiftieth birthday present from the Duke and Duchess of Devonshire in 1998.

The cache-pôt was designed and decorated for The Prince in 2002 by the painter and wood-engraver Jonathan Heale.

The different areas of the garden at Highgrove have evolved over the last twenty-five years, making use of the existing elements (particularly trees and walls) and gradually adding new features. The Prince of Wales commissioned Diana Armfield to paint this view from the kitchen garden in 1988.

The woodland garden evolved in the 1990s, with a Hosta garden and 'Stumpery' designed by Julian and Isabel Bannerman.

Among the new structures at Highgrove is the Sanctuary, a place of natural peace and religious contemplation. The stained-glass windows – inspired by the natural forms in the garden outside – were designed by John Napper shortly before his death in 2001.

The Prince's Trust was founded by His Royal Highness in 1976, using his severance pay from the Royal Navy as a start-up fund. His goal was to encourage young people (aged between 14 and 25) to overcome barriers and get their lives working, in order to realise their potential. Through its nationwide centres, the Trust has helped more than half a million young people since 1976.

The plate above was used at a Gala Dinner for The Prince's Trust, held at Buckingham Palace in March 2003, while that to the left dates from three years later.

The silver disc contains the music played during the 'Party in the Park' in aid of The Prince's Trust in July 2001.

The Trust is the largest of 'The Prince's Charities' – the group of not-for-profit organisations of which His Royal Highness is President. Seventeen of the nineteen charities that make up the group were founded personally by The Prince. The group is the largest multi-cause charitable enterprise in the United Kingdom, and raises over £100 million each year, including the profits from Duchy Originals. The organisations operate across a broad range of activities, including opportunity and enterprise, education, health, the built and natural environments, responsible business, and the arts.

We think every young person has the potential to achieve something in their life.

Annual Review   Prince's Trust

One of those who benefited from the work of The Prince's Trust is the jewellery designer Fiona Rae, who produced these enamel cufflinks decorated with Prince of Wales feathers. She received advice and a £2,400 loan from the Trust in 1991 and is now acknowledged as a leading enamel specialist.

FIONARAE

Since his school days The Prince has been passionate about the British literary tradition and has worked hard to encourage the teaching of English in schools. As President of the Royal Shakespeare Company he made a personal selection from Shakespeare's works, which was published (and broadcast) as *The Prince's Choice* in 1995.

He was introduced to the work of the poet and scholar Kathleen Raine as a young man.

The Prince is also a devotee of the British comic tradition, performing as an undergraduate in a number of productions. In November 1973 he was photographed with Spike Milligan (a particular favourite) at the Eccentrics Club in London.

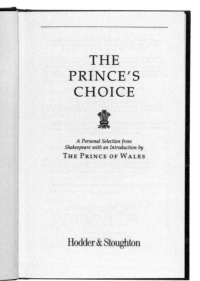

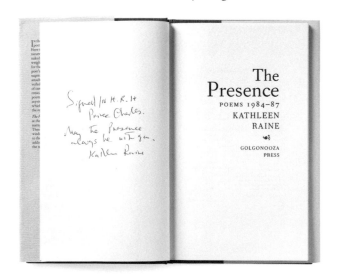

In 2005 Stephen Fry inscribed his book on poetry to The Prince.

The Prince of Wales is a keen patron of music and other performing arts. As a schoolboy he played the cello, and he was a great admirer of the Russian cellist Mstislav Rostropovich. This miniature diamond-set cello was a fiftieth birthday present from Rostropovich to The Prince, who later hosted Rostropovich's seventy-fifth birthday celebrations at Buckingham Palace.

Since 1979 His Royal Highness has been Patron of the Philharmonia Orchestra, who gave him this pair of conductor's batons in 2004.

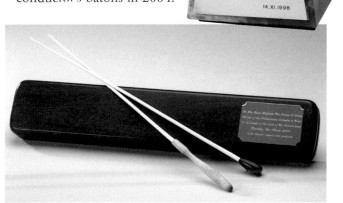

Since 1993 he has been President of the Royal College of Music. The previous President – Queen Elizabeth The Queen Mother – had conferred an Honorary Doctorate of Music on her grandson in 1981.

Sir Anthony Van Dyck
Charles I in three positions, 1635
Oil on canvas

"I can never get over Van Dyck's brilliance in recording character as well as appearance: you feel Charles I really was just like this. Bernini carved his celebrated marble of the King from this three-in-one portrait and the destruction of that bust, in the fire at Whitehall Palace in 1698, was one of the greatest losses to befall the Royal Collection."

This portrait by Susan Crawford – modelled on the Van Dyck of an earlier Charles – was commissioned by The Prince of Wales in 2000 as a hundredth birthday present for his grandmother, Queen Elizabeth The Queen Mother.

The Prince of Wales has a large collection of
Wemyss Ware, which is divided between
Highgrove and Birkhall. The Wemyss factory
was established in Fife in the late nineteenth
century and its success depended very largely
on the design and decorative skills of Karel
Nekola, an immigrant Czech artist responsible
for the decoration on the large fruit bowl.
The commemorative goblet celebrating
Queen Victoria's Diamond Jubilee in 1897
was an early product of the factory.

For The Prince of Wales, the love and collecting of art has been accompanied by increasing proficiency as a practising watercolour artist. He recalls the beginnings, in the early 1970s: 'I'd tried to paint when I was about seven or eight when my father had shown me how to do it with oils. Then, about two years before Ted [Seago] died, I suddenly had a yearning to try with watercolours'. After much persuasion, Seago agreed to teach him: 'he said, "Alright, I'll give you a lesson – but only one."'

Since then, The Prince has worked hard to improve his technique, receiving instruction from John Ward, Bryan Organ and Martin Yeoman, among others. In 1991 a book of his watercolours was published in aid of The Prince's Charities. His work has been exhibited in a number of galleries, including the Royal Academy in London.

The Prince often produces an annotated preparatory study in red ink before working up the finished watercolour in his studio. The view of an abandoned cottage on the island of Stroma, Caithness, was painted in 2003, while that of a Greek mountain range (opposite) is a work of the following year.

His Royal Highness is closely involved in the work of The Prince's Drawing School, founded by him in a converted warehouse in Shoreditch in 2000.

The School runs a broad range of courses concentrating on the teaching of drawing, working on the premise that drawing is a living and evolving language. The small sketchbook shown here is the work of one of the Drawing Year artists.

The Prince's School of Traditional Arts – also based in Shoreditch – aims to teach the arts and crafts skills which have profound roots in all the major faith traditions. It runs courses that combine geometry, wood carving and inlay, Islamic architecture, icon painting, calligraphy, tilemaking, stained glass and mosaic craft.

Through its commercial arm (Traditional Arts Ltd), the School's work is partly self-funding. The coffee cup and saucer – decorated with the 'Praiseworthy' design – is an example of the high-quality goods produced for sale.

Official Opening
of the
Mary Rose Exhibition
by H.R.H. the Prince of Wales

H.M. Naval Base,
Portsmouth
July 9th 1984

Among the many heritage projects with which The Prince has been closely involved is the Mary Rose Trust, of which he is President. In 1975 The Prince spent 47 minutes underwater examining the wreck of the Tudor warship, and during a dive in 1980 he recovered a wooden pulley block from the seabed. This was presented to The Prince when he formally opened the Mary Rose Exhibition in 1984.

Many of The Prince of Wales's views on conservation, planning and architecture were incorporated into his 1988 television documentary *A Vision of Britain*, later published as a book. The English edition appeared in 1989 but many foreign language editions (including Japanese) appeared subsequently. This copy was a present to the Duke of Edinburgh.

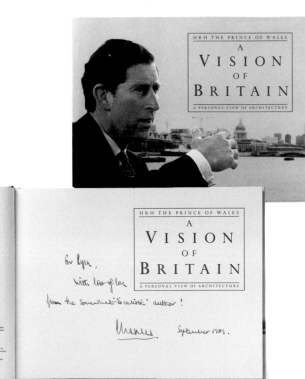

In Poundbury, a development on land belonging to the Duchy of Cornwall outside Dorchester, The Prince challenged late twentieth-century planning assumptions by giving priority to people rather than cars, and by mixing commercial buildings with residential areas, shops and leisure facilities. The Poundbury Masterplan, completed in 1989, incorporated the urban design principles described in *A Vision of Britain*. Construction began in 1993; by the end of 2006 over 1,200 people were living in Poundbury, with 750 people working there too.

Andrew Moore
Silver table, 1698–9
Silver and oak

*"There is something almost irresistible about furniture made of silver: it is so
grand and tremendously rare, and in the case of this table combines a superbly
engraved top with lively sculptural details including the amusing pineapple –
itself a great rarity in those days – on the cross-stretcher underneath."*

The Prince of Wales is involved in a number of architectural conservation projects, ensuring that appropriate uses are found for our nation's historic buildings and that they are saved for future generations. His intervention in late 2007 ensured that Dumfries House in East Ayrshire, designed by the Adam brothers in the 1750s, was saved from a break-up sale. The house still contains its magnificent original furnishings by Thomas Chippendale and contemporary Edinburgh makers and is being opened to the public in 2008.

In his sixtieth birthday year His Royal Highness continues to work ceaselessly to support The Queen and to further his many charitable interests.

Illustrations

In the following list items from the Royal Collection or Royal Archives are prefaced by a crown,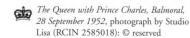

while those from the Collection of HRH The Prince of Wales are prefaced by feathers.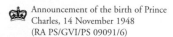

Unless otherwise stated, items in the Royal Collection or Royal Archives are respectively: The Royal Collection © 2008 HM Queen Elizabeth II, and: The Royal Archives © 2008 HM Queen Elizabeth II.

Unless otherwise indicated photography was supplied by The Royal Collection's Picture Library. Royal Collection Enterprises are grateful for permission to reproduce those items listed below for which copyright is not held by The Royal Collection.

EARLY YEARS

Page 5

 The Queen with Prince Charles, Balmoral, 28 September 1952, photograph by Studio Lisa (RCIN 2585018): © reserved

Page 6

 Princess Elizabeth with the infant Prince Charles, 14 December 1948, photograph by Cecil Beaton (RCIN 2999884): © V&A Images/Victoria and Albert Museum

 Flower basket brooch, ?1920s (RCIN 200140)

Page 7

Announcement of the birth of Prince Charles, 14 November 1948 (RA PS/GVI/PS 09091/6)

Crowds outside Buckingham Palace cheer the news of the birth of Prince Charles, 14 November 1948 (RCIN 2814255): © reserved

Page 8

Princess Elizabeth with the infant Prince Charles, Prince Philip, King George VI and Queen Elizabeth, 15 December 1948 (RCIN 2814350): © reserved

The Lily Font, 1840 (RCIN 31741): Crown Copyright; The Royal Collection © 2008 HM Queen Elizabeth II

The book of the baptism service of Prince Charles, calligraphy by Freda Hands, 1948 (RCIN 1080428)

Page 9

Franz Xaver Winterhalter, *The First of May 1851* (oil on canvas; RCIN 406995)

Page 10

Miss Podd putting the finishing touches to Prince Charles's christening cake, 1948 (RCIN 2814358): © reserved

Flowers from the christening cake of Prince Charles, with a note by Queen Mary (RCIN 54845.a, .b)

Silver carousel christening cake decoration, 1948 (RCIN 48958): © reserved

Page 11

Silver-gilt christening cup, made by Thomas Heming, 1773-4 (RCIN 49950)

Leather case containing knife, fork and spoon, *c*.1950 (RCIN 48945): © reserved

Page 12

Princess Elizabeth, Prince Philip and Prince Charles at Clarence House, 1951, photograph by Yousuf Karsh (RCIN 2937627): © Yousuf Karsh/Camera Press

Queen Elizabeth The Queen Mother's copy of *The Tales of Beatrix Potter*, 1902, 1903, 1904 (RCIN 1016641): Beatrix Potter text and illustrations © Frederick Warne & Co., 1902

Prince Charles, 1951, photograph by Marcus Adams (RCIN 2814286)

Page 13

King George VI with Prince Charles, Buckingham Palace, 1951 (RCIN 2937877): © reserved

Prince Charles and Princess Anne in their prams at Clarence House, 1951 (RCIN 2814281): © reserved

Prince Charles's trolley of toy bricks (RCIN 95167): © reserved

Page 14

Prince Charles and Princess Anne with The Queen at Balmoral Castle, 28 September 1952, photographs by Studio Lisa (RCIN 2585014-17): © reserved

The Queen with The Duke of Edinburgh, Princess Anne and Prince Charles at Balmoral, 1953, photograph by James Reid (RCIN 2999886)

Page 15

Prince Charles's Invitation to the Coronation, designed by Joan Hassall, 1953: © reserved

Coronation medal, 1953 (RCIN 441807.b)

The Queen with the Royal Family at Buckingham Palace after the Coronation, 2 June 1953 (RCIN 2937631): © reserved

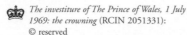
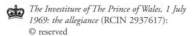

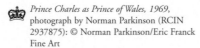

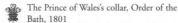
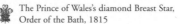
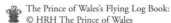

Page 49

The Prince of Wales investing Helen Mirren with the insignia of Dame of the British Empire, 5 December 2003 (RCIN 2937933): Courtesy BCA film

The Order of Merit

Page 50

The Prince of Wales attending Independence celebrations at Albert Park, Fiji, 10 October 1970 (RCIN 2050600): © reserved

Fiji Independence banner (RCIN 2050586): © reserved

Susannah Fiennes, HMY Britannia in Hong Kong Harbour, 1997 (watercolour and bodycolour on grey paper)

Page 51

Mary Anne Aytoun Ellis, Jamaican, 2000 (sepia ink and egg tempera on panel), photography by the National Portrait Gallery

The Prince of Wales's Order of Australia badge

The Prince of Wales visits the Silver Jubilee Agricultural Show, Murwillumbah, Australia, 4 November 1977 (RCIN 2050097): © reserved

Page 52

Ebony box with gold cuff links and tie pin from Ghana, 1961 (RCIN 49235)

Laurens van der Post, A walk with a white bushman, uncorrected proof, 1986

Derek Hill, Sir Laurens van der Post, 1987 (oil on canvas): © HRH The Prince of Wales

Page 53

The Prince of Wales with Nelson Mandela at Mahlamba Ndlopfu, Pretoria, 1 November 1997: © John Stillwell/PA

Robert Wraith, Cape Town, 1997 (pen and ink with watercolour and sepia wash)

Page 54

Johann Zoffany, The Tribuna of the Uffizi, 1772-8 (oil on canvas; RCIN 406983)

Peter Kuhfeld, Loggia dei Lanzi, 1998 (oil on board)

Page 55

The Prince of Wales's Breast Plate of the President of the Republic of Kazakstan

John Sergeant, Prague: Hradčany, 1991 (pen and ink, watercolour and bodycolour)

Emma Sergeant, Leena: Turkmenistan, 1996 (black pencil)

Page 56

Prince of Wales in Indian Headdress, Canada, 1977, photograph by Anwar Hussein (RCIN 2053959): © Anwar Hussein

Leather saddle presented to The Prince of Wales by the Blood Tribe: made by Pete Standing Alone, 1977 (RCIN 94420)

Page 57

President Ronald Reagan and Prince Charles in the Oval Office at the White House, 1 May 1981 (RCIN 2053228): White House official photograph

Crystal bowl on malachite base, 1981

Page 58

Cloak of Napoleon Bonaparte, c.1800 (RCIN 61156)

The Prince of Wales's insignia, Order of St Catherine of Mount Sinai

Emma Sergeant, Head Study, Egypt, 1995 (black pencil)

Page 59

The Prince of Wales's insignia, Order of Mubarak Al Kabir

Gold and quartz model of a desert scene, c.2006

Page 60

Emerald belt of Maharajah Sher Singh, c.1840 (RCIN 11291)

The Prince of Wales in India, November 1980, photograph by Yogendra C. Patel (RCIN 2052844.d): © reserved

FAMILY LIFE

Page 61

The Prince of Wales with Princes William and Harry in the tree house at Highgrove, 6 September 2003, photograph by Mario Testino (RCIN 2937880): © Mario Testino

Page 62

Michael Noakes, Portrait of HM The Queen, 1972-73 (oil on board)

Bryan Organ, Study for a portrait of The Duke of Edinburgh, 1983 (watercolour and bodycolour): © Bryan Organ

A nest of silver boxes engraved with views of royal residences, designed and made by Gerald Benney, 1972 (RCIN 95749)

Page 63

Chirstmas card depicting the Royal Family with Prince Edward as a baby, 1965 (RCIN 2937883): © reserved

Prince Charles with Prince Edward on a go-cart, 1969 (RCIN 2942637): © reserved

The Prince of Wales, The Old Man of Lochnagar, 1980

Page 64

Sir Edwin Landseer, Hector, Nero and Dash with the parrot, Lorry, 1838 (oil on canvas; RCIN 405969)

Prince Charles at Balmoral Castle with his labrador, Harvey, 1978 (RCIN 2936098): © reserved

Page 65

Cast bronze figure of Tigga, made by Angela Conner, 1995

Sir Edwin Landseer, Eos, 1841 (oil on canvas; RCIN 403219)

Page 66

George Stubbs, The Prince of Wales's Phaeton, 1793 (oil on canvas; RCIN 400994)

The Prince of Wales riding Allibar at the Clun Chase, Ludlow, October 1980: © reserved

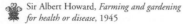
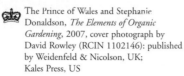
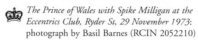
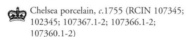